The MINDFUL STEPS Series

BIG BROTHER

A MINDFUL HOW-TO GUIDE FOR TODDLERS AND KIDS

Written and Illustrated by
Andrea Dorn, MSW, LISW-CP

For Henry

**And for caregivers, everywhere, who are
out in the trenches, doing their very best.**

A special thank you to my family and to all those who contributed to the creation of this book.

Oh! Hi, there! What is your name?

Really?! That is **MY** name, too!

I am growing every day, and as I grow,
I get to learn lots of fun things!

Optional Question: What fun things do YOU know how to do?

My family is growing too
and one fun thing I am learning
is how to be a **BIG** brother!

Optional Questions: How many people are in your family?
Who else do you know that is a big brother?

Here is what happens when a new baby comes.

First, our baby will grow inside my mommy's tummy.

(I also used to be a baby inside my mommy's tummy!)

Optional Questions: Do you have any pictures or videos of you inside your mommy's tummy? Sometimes mommies have more than one baby growing in their tummy. How many babies are growing in YOUR mommy's tummy?

As our baby grows, Mommy's tummy will get
bigger and bigger.

("Hello in there, baby!")

While our baby is growing inside Mommy's tummy,
we will get ready for our baby to meet us!

We will make a special space for our baby to sleep.

(I have a special space to sleep, too!)

Optional Questions: Where is your special place to sleep? Where will your baby sleep?

And we will get the things our baby needs!

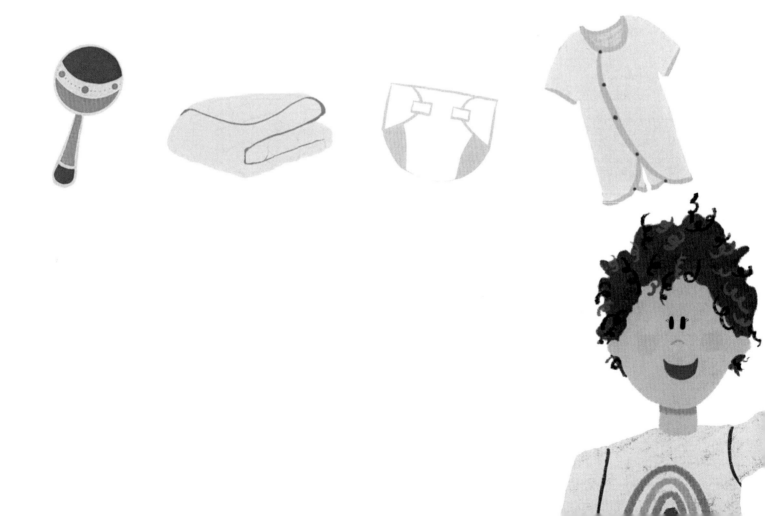

One day our baby will be ready to
come out of Mommy's tummy.

My mommy will go to a place
called a hospital so the new baby
can come out to meet us!

The hospital has special people called doctors and nurses.
They will help our baby come out of Mommy's tummy.

Mommy will stay in the hospital for a few days.

Optional Question: Some mommies have their new baby at home. Where will your mommy have your new baby?

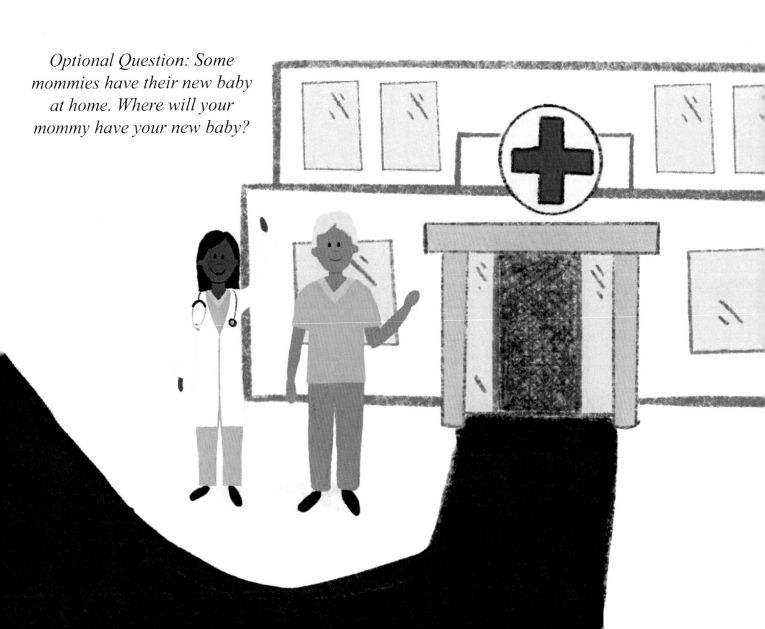

I might miss my mommy when she is gone
(she will miss me, too!),
but she will come home very soon.

I will stay home and keep getting ready for
our new baby.

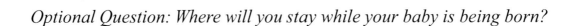

Optional Question: Where will you stay while your baby is being born?

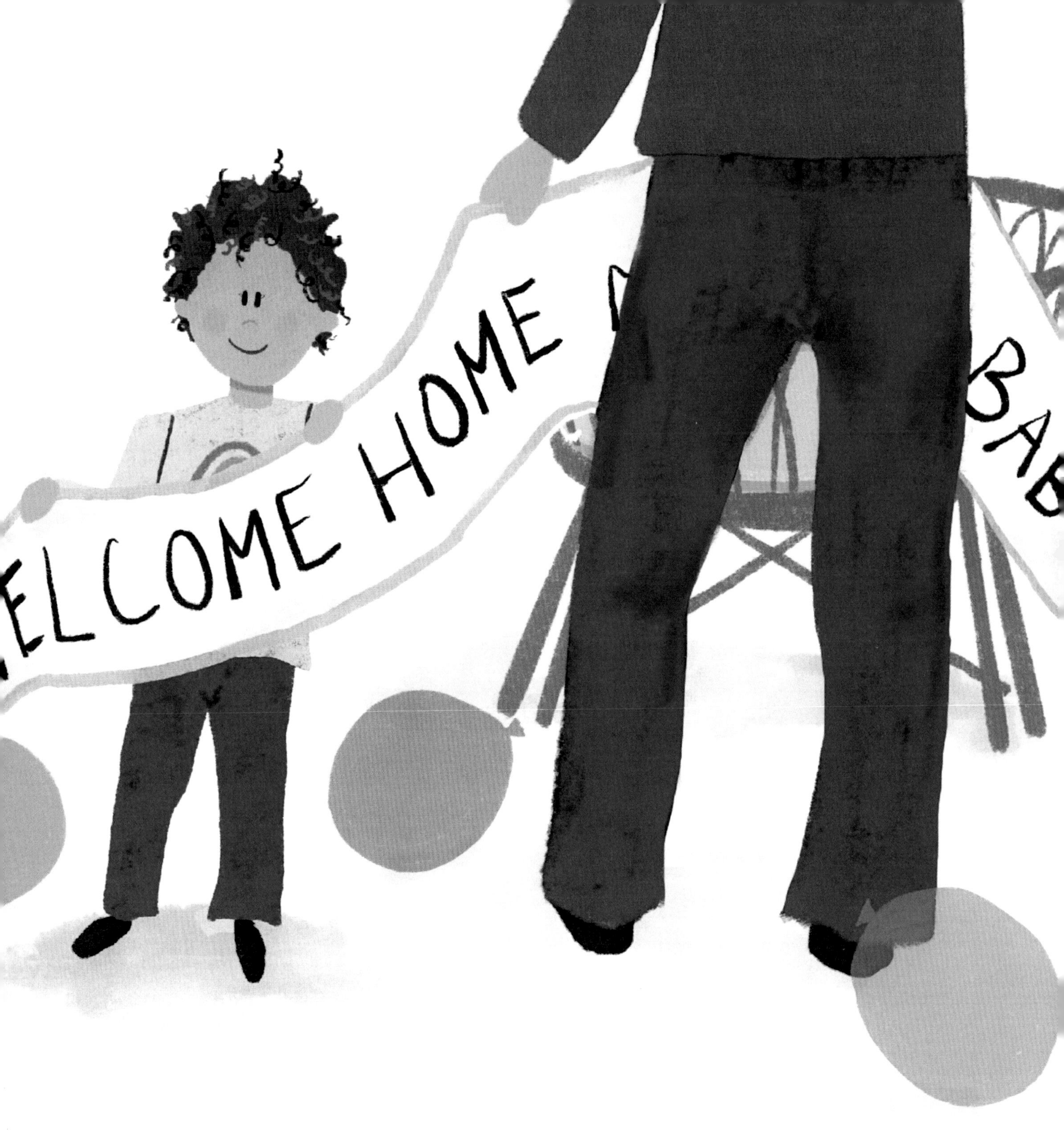
ELCOME HOME
BAB

Then, I will meet our new baby.

Our new baby is so cute and little!

Optional Questions: Do you know what your new baby's name will be?
How do you feel about meeting your new baby?

At first, our baby will just eat and sleep most of the time.

Our baby cannot talk,
so it will cry to tell us it needs something.

We can change our baby's diaper,
feed our baby, and sing songs to our baby to help it feel better.

I am a big brother, so I can be a big helper with our new baby!

There, that's better!

Optional Questions: What other things can you do to help your new baby?
How do you feel when you are a big helper?

I am also learning how to calm my body so I can be
gentle with our new baby.

My body is calm when it is quiet, kind, still,
and does good listening.

("shhhhh")

I can use my calm body to have gentle hands and feet and a quiet voice around our baby.

Optional Questions: Will you show me your gentle hands and feet and quiet voice?
Where is it ok to touch the baby?

A baby will bring big changes at our house.
Sometimes, I might feel sad or mad when the people I love
can't play with me right away, or when I have to be quiet,
or share, or when our baby cries...

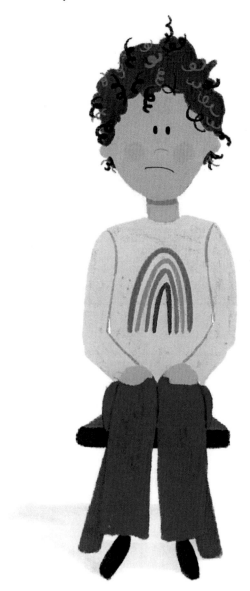

It can be **very** loud!

Optional Question: Do you ever feel mad or sad around your new baby?

I can find a special place to go when I feel mad or sad.
I can stop and take a deep breath to notice how my body
and my heart feel.

Optional Questions: Where is your special place? What do you need when you feel mad or sad?
(Sometimes I need a hug, to stomp my feet, or to play with some toys.)

I can remember it is ok to feel upset.

I can remember I will always be very special to
the people who love me.

I can use words to tell people how I feel or ask them for help.

I can remember that I am a big kid,
and I can do all kinds of fun things
that babies can't do!

Optional Question: What fun things can you do that the baby can't do yet?

Our new baby will grow just like me,
and I can teach our baby everything I know!

Optional Question: What fun things would you like to teach your baby?

We will be best friends.

Growing up is so much fun,
especially when I have someone to grow with!

See you next time!

Big Brother Meditation

Life is full of change, you see.
But one thing that won't change is your love for me.

A new baby is (coming/here), so cute and so new.
(I'll be/I am) a big brother with so much to do!

I'll use my quiet voice and kind hands and feet.
If I feel mad or sad a deep breath will help me.

I'll teach our new baby all that I know.
It will be so much fun to learn and to grow.

Caregiver Guided Meditation

Take a moment to pause and focus on your breath. Close your eyes and breathe deeply and slowly in through your nose and out through your mouth. Pay close attention to the way your breath feels as it enters your nose and fills your lungs. As you exhale, let go of any tension in the muscles of your body.
Take this time to focus solely on this one moment. In this moment, give your child(ren) and yourself the gift of validation and acceptance. A new baby is a time for many emotions, all of which are normal. As you breathe and center yourself, acknowledge how you are feeling in this moment. Continue breathing deeply and focus your intentions for yourself on the phrases of this take of a "loving-kindness" or "metta" meditation:

May I feel connected and calm.
May I be patient and gentle with my children and myself.
May I keep joy and laughter in all that I do.
May I be present in the easy and uneasy times.
May I begin each moment with gratitude, acceptance, and willingness.

Repeat one or all of these phrases as many times as you need and as often as you need as a way to remind yourself to connect and care for yourself.

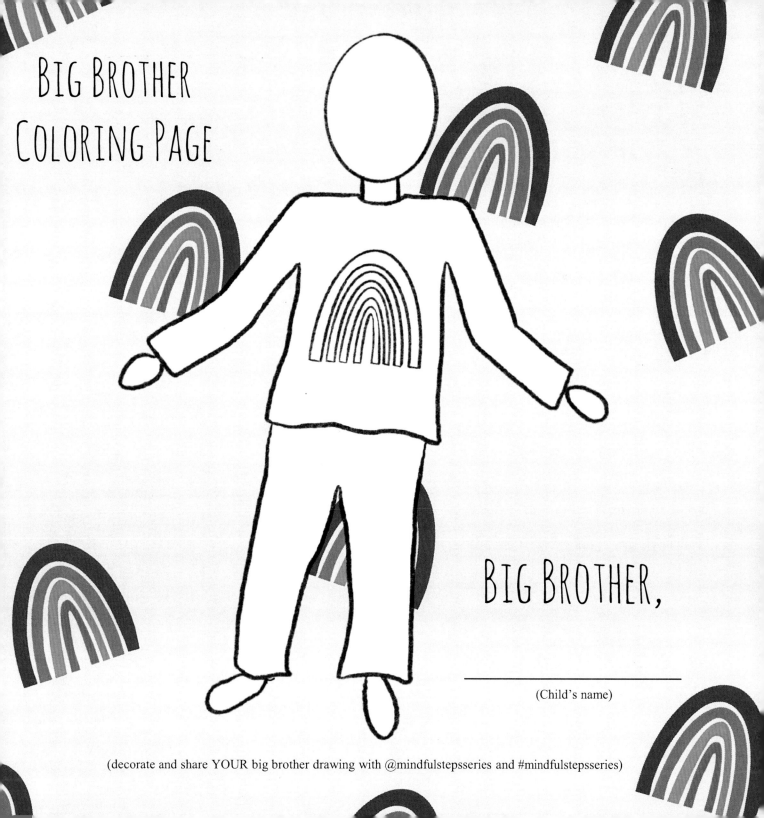

Big Brother
Coloring Page

Big Brother,

_____

(Child's name)

(decorate and share YOUR big brother drawing with @mindfulstepsseries and #mindfulstepsseries)

Especially for Parents and Caregivers
How to use this book:

Dear Caregiver,

Congratulations on the new baby in your life! Whether you are expecting a new baby or it has already arrived, a new addition to the family can be a time of many emotions. How can mindfulness assist in this process? In his book, *Wherever You Go, There You Are,* Jon Kabat-Zinn defines mindfulness as "paying attention in a particular way: on purpose, in the present moment, and nonjudgmentally." Mindfulness also often includes attempting to let go of any attachments we have to expectations and desired outcomes in a moment, and encourages us to live each new moment with curiosity and gratitude. The arrival of a new baby is a beautiful time, but can also often be a sleepless, chaotic, and vulnerable time where we are exposed to a multitude of judgments and expectations (both from ourselves and others!). Mindfulness and mindful parenting can be effective tools to help us neutralize ineffective judgments and expectations. Mindfulness can also help ground us and our children in the present and inspire connection with, and gratitude for, others and any moment that comes our way.

For children, a new baby is also a time of confusing and exciting change and every child processes this change a bit differently. One way to assist your child in navigating a new baby is to help prepare him for what to expect and to validate any grief he may feel at the loss of his life as he knew it (this grief can sometimes appear at confusing times and is often behavioral). This book is designed to read with your child often, both before and after the birth of your baby, to talk about the steps of welcoming a new baby into your home, to teach ways to cope with and encourage discussion about big emotions, and to celebrate becoming a big brother. Visit andreadorn.com for resources and more Mindful Steps series books!

Warmest regards and again, congratulations on the new addition to your family!
Andrea

Tip: This book is about more than just learning about becoming a big brother. To reinforce emotional intelligence and awareness, ask open-ended questions while reading each page. Focus on creating questions that relate to your situation and deepen emotional understanding and coping skills. Examples of this include: "How does the child in the story feel when the baby is born?" or "What can the child in the story say if he thinks the baby is crying too loud?" You can also use some of the suggested interactive prompts at the bottom of the pages to spark conversation and to help foster good attachment and communication about feelings and individuality. Depending on the age and development of your child, he may not always have the answers, but it will help him to start thinking about the importance of these concepts.

Tips for helping kids with new siblings:

- **Prepare your child:** Preparation for the new baby can begin long before the baby arrives. Examples of ways to prepare your child include: talking about the new baby, reading this book, listening to recordings of babies crying, practicing being gentle, pointing out other babies and older siblings, and allowing your child time to learn to play independently. These activities will give your child's brain some time to prepare for and adjust to some of the changes that will come with a new baby under less stressful conditions.

    *Note: Children aged 2 and under may have a more difficult time conceptualizing this information, but talking about what to expect will help to prime their brain to be more ready to connect the dots.

- **Include your child:** Before the baby is born, offer ways your child can help prepare for the baby's arrival. This can include anything from helping decorate the baby's room, to picking out the baby's name, to shopping for things the new baby will need. Calling the baby "our baby" can also help to create a sense of inclusion and ownership of the title "big brother." After the baby is born, allow your child (when they wish) to be involved in taking care of the new baby with your help. This can include singing to the baby during feedings to helping throw away diapers after a changing. Be creative about how your child can assume the new role of "big helper."

- **Prepare the environment:** Help your child create a special place that is just for him. Allow your child to keep toys that are just for him. Though sharing is an important skill to learn, it is natural for children (and adults, for that matter!) to want to be in control of some of their belongings and spaces. If your child needs to give up a bed or his room, try to make this transition several months before the baby arrives (when possible).

- **Connect:** Build attachment with your child by connecting as often as you can. Attempt to carve out special times for you to dedicate your undivided attention to each of your children individually. This is important to do in general, but especially after the baby is born.

- **Routine:** Try to stick with the routine your child is used to as best as you can. Additionally, to the best of your ability, try not to make too many other significant changes during the period surrounding your new baby's birth (examples of significant changes include: potty training, moving, or changing schools).

- **Understanding, validation, and healthy boundaries:** It is *very* common for children to exhibit aggressive or regressive behaviors after a new baby is born. Oftentimes, these behaviors come from big feelings that your child is unsure how to process. Research shows that helping your child process these big emotions by doing your best to validate your child's feelings before offering any kind of correction or discipline can help reduce the behaviors more quickly. Try to hold a space for your child to feel whatever he feels in the moment without attempting to persuade him to feel differently. Allow your child to become more regulated before offering any kind of discipline or consequence. Reacting with kindness and love will build attachment and security which are very important factors in early child development. Though connection is important, so are healthy boundaries, so be sure to enforce things like gentle touches when necessary.

- **Your role:** Mindful parenting requires intentionally being in the moment without judgement. If/when difficult situations arise, practice being gentle with yourself and with your child. Model taking slow, deep breaths, take a short break, and/or remind yourself that this is a process that may take some time. Remembering to intentionally take time for yourself is also important for family and self-care. Though it may not always seem like it, kids will benefit and learn from your ability to calm your own body and regulate your emotions. Everything is a phase; every day is a new day. Rest in knowing you are doing your best in each moment and so is your child.

Made in United States
North Haven, CT
17 November 2024